PROPERTY OF
WEST GREY PUBLIC LIBRARY

EXPLORING COUNTRIES

Switzerland

by Derek Zobel

BLASTOFF! READERS
5

BELLWETHER MEDIA • MINNEAPOLIS, MN

Note to Librarians, Teachers, and Parents:

Blastoff! Readers are carefully developed by literacy experts and combine standards-based content with developmentally appropriate text.

Level 1 provides the most support through repetition of high-frequency words, light text, predictable sentence patterns, and strong visual support.

Level 2 offers early readers a bit more challenge through varied simple sentences, increased text load, and less repetition of high-frequency words.

Level 3 advances early-fluent readers toward fluency through increased text and concept load, less reliance on visuals, longer sentences, and more literary language.

Level 4 builds reading stamina by providing more text per page, increased use of punctuation, greater variation in sentence patterns, and increasingly challenging vocabulary.

Level 5 encourages children to move from "learning to read" to "reading to learn" by providing even more text, varied writing styles, and less familiar topics.

Whichever book is right for your reader, Blastoff! Readers are the perfect books to build confidence and encourage a love of reading that will last a lifetime!

This edition first published in 2011 by Bellwether Media, Inc.

No part of this publication may be reproduced in whole or in part without written permission of the publisher. For information regarding permission, write to Bellwether Media, Inc., Attention: Permissions Department, 5357 Penn Avenue South, Minneapolis, MN 55419.

Library of Congress Cataloging-in-Publication Data
Zobel, Derek, 1983-
  Switzerland / by Derek Zobel.
    p. cm. – (Exploring countries) (Blastoff! readers)
  Includes bibliographical references and index.
  Summary: "Developed by literacy experts for students in grades three through seven, this book introduces young readers to the geography and culture of Switzerland"–Provided by publisher.
  ISBN 978-1-60014-577-3 (hardcover : alk. paper)
  1. Switzerland–Juvenile literature. I. Title.
  DQ17.Z63 2011
  949.4-dc22   2010041168

Text copyright © 2011 by Bellwether Media, Inc. BLASTOFF! READERS and associated logos are trademarks and/or registered trademarks of Bellwether Media, Inc.

Printed in the United States of America, North Mankato, MN.

010111   1176

Contents

France

Did you know?
The official name of Switzerland is the Swiss Confederation. It was formed in 1291, which makes it one of the oldest countries in Europe.

Switzerland is a country in the center of Europe. It is divided into 26 **cantons** and covers 15,937 square miles (41,277 square kilometers). Its borders with five surrounding countries are formed by land features.

Germany, Austria, and Liechtenstein touch the northeastern part of Switzerland. The southern part of the country borders Italy, and France lies to the west. Switzerland's capital is Bern.

Switzerland is a **landlocked** country. Its landscape includes two major mountain ranges and a large **plateau**. In the north, the Jura Mountains run along the borders with France and Germany. South of the Jura range is the Central Plateau, often called the Swiss Plateau. Most Swiss people live on this flat land.

fun fact

The Matterhorn is a famous peak in the Swiss Alps. Many people enjoy the challenge of trying to climb this dangerous mountain.

The Swiss Alps are found in southern Switzerland. They are part of a larger mountain range that runs through southern Europe. Two major rivers start in the Swiss Alps. The Rhine River flows north from Switzerland, through Germany, and into the North Sea. The Rhône River travels south through France and empties into the Mediterranean Sea.

The largest lake in Switzerland is Lake Geneva, or *Lac Léman*. It is located in southwestern Switzerland and southeastern France. The lake covers 224 square miles (580 square kilometers), and its deepest point is 1,017 feet (310 meters). It is one of the largest and deepest lakes in western Europe.

Over thousands of years, large **glaciers** melted as temperatures rose. The melted ice formed Lake Geneva. The Rhône River, flowing down through the Swiss Alps, feeds the lake. It branches off near the Swiss city of Geneva.

fun fact

People have found the remains of ancient houses and other buildings on Lake Geneva's shores. These remains are thousands of years old!

lynx

Did you know?
The lynx disappeared from Switzerland in the early 20th century. People have recently reintroduced it, and there are now about 100 lynx in the country.

The mountains of Switzerland are home to a variety of animals. Roe deer, ibexes, and mountain sheep roam the rocky terrain. Foxes wander the area and try to sneak up on Alpine marmots. These marmots, which look like groundhogs, must also watch out for **raptors** like booted and golden eagles.

bearded
vulture

Alpine
marmot

Alpine
salamander

fun fact
The Alpine salamander lives in Switzerland. It gives birth to live young instead of laying eggs. Females can be pregnant for three years before they give birth!

Bearded vultures soar above the Swiss Alps. These **scavengers**, known as "bone crushers," eat the bones of dead animals. Blackbirds, swans, robins, and woodpeckers also fly throughout the country.

! **fun fact**
The traditional clothes of the
Swiss people often have
detailed designs and patterns.

Over 7.5 million people live in Switzerland.
The people identify themselves as Swiss, but they
come from many different backgrounds. Switzerland
has a very **diverse** population because of its
location between Germany, Italy, and France.

Switzerland has four official languages. German **dialects** are spoken by people in the regions of Switzerland near Germany, Austria, and Liechtenstein. Swiss people near the Italian border speak Italian, and those who live close to France speak French. The fourth official language, Romansh, is spoken by people who live in eastern Switzerland.

Speak German!

Swiss German varies throughout Switzerland. There is no one dialect, but they are all based on traditional German.

English	German	How to say it
hello	hallo	HA-low
good-bye	auf wiedersehen	owf VEE-der-zay-en
yes	ja	yah
no	nein	nine
please	bitte	BIT-tuh
thank you	danke	DAHN-kah
friend	Freund	froind

Most Swiss people live on the Central Plateau.
This region has many large cities, including Bern, Zürich,
and Geneva. Many people who live in the cities have
apartments, although some own houses. People use cars,
buses, and trains to get around. They buy food and other
goods at open-air markets, small stores, and supermarkets.

In the countryside, people live in houses in small villages or on farms. They shop at local stores in their villages. When they want to go to a city, they take trains or drive their cars.

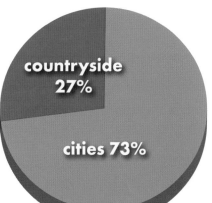

countryside 27%

cities 73%

Schools vary throughout Switzerland's 26 cantons, but all children must attend school for nine years. People from each canton meet to try to make their school standards the same.

Most students in Switzerland go to preschool. Then they attend the nine required years of school. This includes elementary school, where they learn reading, writing, math, science, and other subjects. It also includes several years of secondary school. Students who complete secondary school can go to a university.

fun fact

Some Swiss students do apprenticeships. They learn skills from professionals while they also attend secondary school. When they graduate, they can begin full-time work.

Where People Work in Switzerland

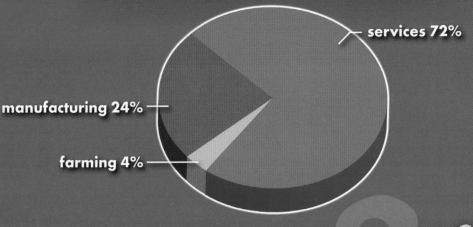

services 72%

manufacturing 24%

farming 4%

Did you know?

Switzerland uses its rivers to create power. The rivers flow through power plants and spin turbines to generate electricity.

fun fact

The Swiss are known for the watches they make. Some watches made in Switzerland sell for thousands of dollars!

In Switzerland's cities, most people have **service jobs**. They work in government offices, restaurants, and stores. Highly skilled workers have jobs in Switzerland's famous banks. People from around the world keep their money in Swiss banks.

In the countryside, farmers work the land to grow wheat, oats, and other grains. They also grow many fruits and vegetables. Some farmers raise cattle, chicken, and pigs. The milk from dairy cows is used to make cream, chocolate, and cheese.

The Swiss enjoy many outdoor activities and sports. Skiers, snowboarders, and hikers love to explore the slopes of the Swiss Alps. Adventurous people go **mountaineering** to try to reach mountain peaks. On Switzerland's lakes, people enjoy windsurfing, sailing, and fishing.

Did you know?

Alpine horns are long, wooden horns played by people throughout Switzerland. The horns were originally used for communication between mountain peaks.

Ice hockey is one of the biggest sports in Switzerland. Most Swiss people support one of the teams in the Swiss professional league. Many Swiss people play soccer for local teams. Most are fans of the national team, which often goes to the **World Cup**.

fun fact

In Switzerland, the average person consumes about 22 pounds (10 kilograms) of chocolate every year!

The German, French, and Italian regions of Switzerland are known for many different dishes. Sausages and potatoes are common in the German region. *Röschti* is a dish where shredded potatoes are fried in a pan. Pasta and pizza are favorites in the Italian region. The French region has made **quiche** popular throughout Switzerland.

Two of the most famous foods from Switzerland are cheese and chocolate. Emmental, Gruyère, and other cheeses are popular around the world. Swiss chocolate is sent to countries throughout Europe and North America.

röschti

quiche

Unspunnenfest

Most holidays in Switzerland are unique to each canton. There are only a few national holidays. Swiss National Day falls on August 1 and celebrates the formation of Switzerland in 1291. On January 1, the Swiss celebrate New Year's Day. Families gather together to eat large dinners and give each other gifts.

The other two holidays celebrated in all of the cantons are the Christian holidays **Ascension Day** and Christmas. Easter, another Christian holiday, is important in all but one canton. Many Swiss families go to church on these holidays.

fun fact

Many towns in Switzerland hold their own festivals. Interlaken holds Unspunnenfest once every ten years to celebrate Swiss culture and history.

Red Cross headquarters

Did you know?

The symbol of the Red Cross is a red cross on a white background, which is the opposite of Switzerland's flag.

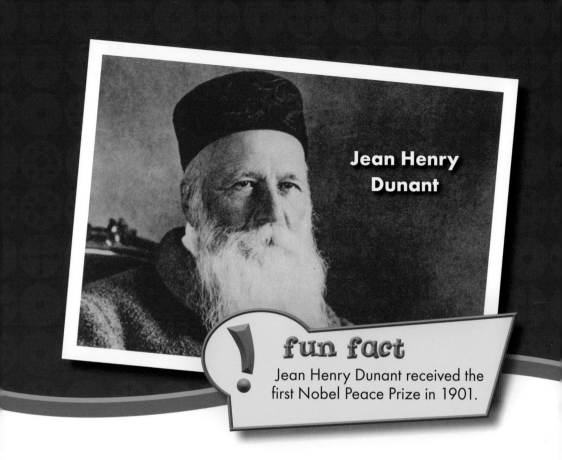

Jean Henry
Dunant

! fun fact

Jean Henry Dunant received the first Nobel Peace Prize in 1901.

Switzerland has been a **neutral** country for much of its history. During times of war, Switzerland has not chosen to fight. Instead, the Swiss try to help those hurt by war.

In the 19th century, a Swiss businessman named Jean Henry Dunant saw a battle in Italy. He was shocked by the lack of medical care for the wounded troops on both sides of the fight. When he went back to Switzerland, he and a few others founded a group to help people affected by war. This group, the **International Committee of the Red Cross**, keeps the Swiss tradition of helping others alive today.

Fast Facts About Switzerland

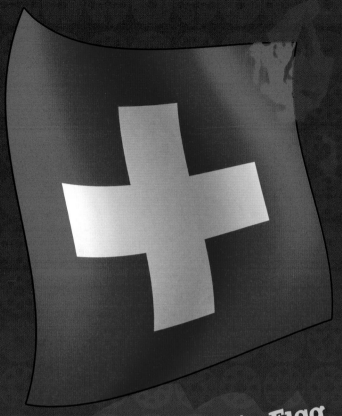

Switzerland's Flag

The flag of Switzerland is one of only two square-shaped flags in the world. It is red with a white cross in the middle. It was adopted on December 12, 1889.

Official Name: Swiss Confederation

Area: 15,937 square miles
(41,277 square kilometers);
Switzerland is the 135th
largest country in the world.

Capital City:	Bern
Important Cities:	Zürich, Geneva
Population:	7,623,438 (July 2010)
Official Languages:	German, French, Italian, Romansh
National Holiday:	Swiss National Day (August 1)
Religions:	Christian (79.3%), Other/None (16.4%), Muslim (4.3%)
Major Industries:	banking, farming, manufacturing, services
Natural Resources:	salt, sand, gravel, marble
Manufactured Products:	machinery, watches, chemicals, metals, food products
Farm Products:	barley, oats, wheat, cattle, chickens, pigs
Unit of Money:	Swiss franc; the franc is divided into 100 centimes.

Glossary

Ascension Day—the day in the Christian calendar that marks when Jesus Christ ascended into heaven

cantons—states of Switzerland; Switzerland has 26 cantons.

dialects—unique ways of speaking a language; dialects are often specific to certain regions of a country.

diverse—made up of different parts; the Swiss people are diverse because they come from German, Italian, French, Romansh, and other backgrounds.

glaciers—massive sheets of ice that cover large land areas

International Committee of the Red Cross—a group based in Switzerland that helps war victims throughout the world; the Red Cross provides food and medical care for the victims.

landlocked—surrounded by land; Switzerland does not border any major bodies of water.

mountaineering—the sport of climbing mountains

neutral—not taking a side

plateau—an area of flat, raised land

quiche—a pie made from eggs and milk; quiche is often filled with vegetables and meat.

raptors—birds that hunt other animals for food; eagles and hawks are types of raptors.

scavengers—animals that feed on the bodies of dead animals

service jobs—jobs that perform tasks for people or businesses

World Cup—an international soccer competition held every four years

To Learn More

AT THE LIBRARY

Güdel, Helen. *Dear Alexandra: A Story of Switzerland*. Norwalk, Conn.: Soundprints, 1999.

Harris, Pamela K., and Brad Clemmons. *Welcome to Switzerland*. Mankato, Minn.: Child's World, 2008.

Rogers Seavey, Lura. *Switzerland*. New York, N.Y.: Children's Press, 2001.

ON THE WEB

Learning more about Switzerland is as easy as 1, 2, 3.

1. Go to www.factsurfer.com.

2. Enter "Switzerland" into the search box.

3. Click the "Surf" button and you will see a list of related Web sites.

With factsurfer.com, finding more information is just a click away.

Index

PROPERTY OF
WEST GREY PUBLIC LIBRARY

The images in this book are reproduced through the courtesy of: Henry Wilson, front cover, pp. 6-7, 7 (small), 11 (top), 14, 15, 23 (top and bottom); Maisei Raman, front cover (flag), p. 28; Jon Eppard, pp. 4-5; Jon Arnold / Photolibrary, p. 8; Bärtschi Daniel / Age Fotostock, p. 9; Jasper Doest / Minden Pictures, pp. 10-11; Roberto Cerruti, p. 11 (middle); imagebroker rf / Photolibrary, p. 12; Christian Kober / Photolibrary, pp. 12, 24-25; Michael Peuckert / Photolibrary, pp. 16-17; Henk Meijer / Alamy, p. 18; Brian Summers / Photolibrary, p. 19 (left); Igor Gratzer, p. 19 (right); David Epperson / Getty Images, p. 20; Bachman Bachman / Photolibrary, p. 21; Fuse / Getty Images, p. 22; Guenter Fischer / Photolibrary, p. 26; Time & Life Pictures / Getty Images, p. 27; Jeff Banke, p. 29 (bill); Sorin Popa, p. 29 (coin).